THE ADVENTURE OF
LEVI AND JUDAH
LION OF THE TRIBE OF JUDAH

BABA THANKS

authorHOUSE®

AuthorHouse™
1663 Liberty Drive
Bloomington, IN 47403
www.authorhouse.com
Phone: 1-800-839-8640

Published by AuthorHouse 6/17/2013

ISBN: 978-1-4772-4605-4 (sc)
ISBN: 978-1-4772-4606-1 (e)

ACKNOWLEDGEMENTS

First I acknowledge my Lord and my God for all He has done for me in my life, His Love, His Teaching, His Understanding. Better to be of an humble spirit with the lowly, than to divide the spoil with the proud.

Second I would like to thank my blood brother for all his help and understanding, his contribution in my life, I owe no man nothing but love.

Thridly I thank Author House and their staffs for all their work in helping me, getting this book out.

fourth I thank the book sellers for putting this books on their websites and book stores.

Fifth I thank AJ Design for designing the cover of this book, your vision was God sent.

AUTHOR'S NOTE

   Life, itself is an adventure, so to be able to write things down to help this and the next generation is GOD gift.

   This book is not a book based on fiction but on reality, it is not a book to excite your senses, but to show you what's really happening in the world of today.

   My LORD and my GOD once said, a man's enemy is a member of his house hold. Your house hold does not always mean the family you are born into, it can also mean your religious family, friends, race, gender, etc.

   The experience in this book are experience I have gone through in the flesh and also in the spirit, I once heard a preacher say, if you give your life to GOD, you would not go through any problems in life but what the preacher should have said was that, if you give your life to GOD he would help you over come all life adventure.

   GOD would be your rock and in His palm would you be.

   This life adventure has shown me that a person needs the GOD of Adam in their life, to say you don't, well that is the adventure of your life.

No matter what circumstance you are in, nothing can shut GOD out of your life. As long as your heart is right towards Him and towards others, GOD will not forsake you.

Contents

INTRODUCTION 1

ANGEL 5

KIDS ON ICE 7

NUN 9

PLANE FLEW 11

GOLDEN CALF 13

CHILDREN OF ABEL 15

HANDS IN HEAVEN 16

THREE O'CLOCK 19

WITH A BRANCH 21

MONEY 23

BEGGAR 24

MAN AT THE GATE 26

BRETHREN 29

BUSINESS 30

WATER 33

RICH MAN 34

MY PEOPLE 36

EGYPTIAN 37

SABBATH DAY   38

O MAN OF GOD   43

STOREHOUSE   44

ARE YOU A CHRISTIAN   46

O MIGHTY MAN   48

MONITOR   49

FLY ON THE WALL   52

WHILE MEN SLEPT   53

JEZEBAL   55

PHARAOH   57

POLICE MEN   59

BRO, HE IS MY HERO   61

WHAT I THINK OF YOU
AND YOUR GOD   63

DELIVERANCE   65

MY LORD SAID OWE NO
MAN NOTHING BUT LOVE   67

PRAYER   69

CONCLUSION   71

OTHER BOOKS BY THE SAME AUTHOR

HOW CAN I
– ISBN 9781456782795

This book is about a young man who befriend a young lady, who had problems in her life and he tried to help her understand what she was passing through by using the word and love of God, but because he would not join himself with her, she started to use craft against him.

INTRODUCTION

What a day in heaven, tears on the faces of everyone, the harp and trumpet played to get everyone in the mood of happiness, but the residents in heaven were lossing their beloved. The sound of their voices wouldn't be heard for a time, a time and a half, even though it was only for a short time in heaven, but their presence always put a smile on everybody's face.

It was time for them to be men and explore the earth, knowing where they are going was full of trials and tribulations, they were given to two gate keepers on earth, until they were ready to leave alone.

The lessons the gate keepers, taught them was a reminder of what their father had taught them before they left heaven, teaching of wisdom, understanding, humbleness, and love which is GOD. The gate keepers, would always say remember the sons of who you are, remember your father's name.

As they left their home in heaven, they walked pass the street of light, which was a long road with light coming from every part even from the ground.

With every step they took the light got brighter, leading them in one direction, looking back was not an option and they heard their father's voice which said **"Remember You Are The Sons Of THE GREAT KING"**.

LION OF THE TRIBE
OF JUDAH

ANGEL

Once upon a time there was two brother's, one called Levi and the other one called Judah.

They were both at the entrance of Judah house with their niece and nephews, just about to open the front door, when Judah looked up and saw something flying in the air and he said to his niece and nephews. What is that flying and they replied uncle, it's an angel and this angel was dressed in all white.

The angel stopped in the air, looked down at all of them, and smiled, but just behind the angel that was dressed in white was something else flying, but this one was dressed in black.

At first it was one then two dressed in black. Judah tried to open the front door quickly, and as it opened.

Levi, Judah, their niece and nephews all ran inside the house and Judah shut the door. Levi took the children into the living room, while Judah and the angel dressed in white stayed in the hall way and they both got down on their kneels.

Looking through the glass on the front door, Judah

and the angel saw a shadow appear at the door. The shadow first, knocked on the door softly but they did not answer it and then it knocked the second time, but this time a little harder, and they still did not answer and then it knocked again the third time and the whole house shook.

Levi and the children now came close towards Judah and the angel, but with his hands, Judah signed for them all to get down on the floor.

They all got closer together and the angel in white said, I have been sent to you by Nun to protect you and if you ever need me, just call on Nun and I will come to you.

Who is Nun asked Levi and with a tinkle in his eyes and a smile, the angel said. Nun is the Beginning and the End, the Alpha and Omega, He is our Father in Heaven, Hallowed be His name in Heaven and on Earth. He is JEHOVAH.

I am here to guide you through the gates into the city, but outside this door are bad dogs, those who lie in words and deeds.

You should never open the door for anyone that you don't know, because when you open the door for the evil one, you have giving him a way to come into your life and he will use that door to do bad things to you or the members of your family.

The dark shadow at the front door disappeared and light came into the house.

KIDS ON ICE

It was a very cold day, all the roads were very icy, snow was falling and it covered all the parked cars on the streets.

Looking outside of the window Levi and Judah saw a car reversing, but as the car was about to drive away in front was a little girl hanging on the car grille with one hand, as the car drove off, the girl was on the road and Levi and Judah ran outside to help her.

Levi ran back into the house to call the ambulance and Judah was about to pick her up when he looked up and saw a second body down the hill but because it was so cold, Judah picked her up, went into the house and laid her down next to the open fire in the living room.

Just about to go out again to pick up the other body when Levi said to Judah. Where are you going the ambulance is on the way. There is another body down the hill said Judah and he ran out and picked up the body and laid it next to the open fire.

At this time Levi had collected some blankets and

covered the two bodies to keep them warm, he also got a bucket of warm water and some towels.

Levi dipped the towels into the warm water and placed them on the foreheads of the two bodies to help warm them up.

All of a sudden a bit of the flame flew out and hit the carpet, but Judah quickly put it out by pouring the bucket of warm water on it. At this time the second body got up and it was a young boy about the age of seven years old.

NUN

Nun was clothed with a garment down to the foot and girt about the paps with a golden girdle He crossed His hands, place them upon the heads of Levi and Judah and placed a blessing on them.

To you Levi, I have given the priesthood and I am your inheritance, therefore he who bless thee shall be blessed but to the man that curse thee, the devil shall be at his doorstep and that man shall perish.

Righteousness a crown upon your head, understanding your breastplate, truth and faithfulness your garment and prophesy your ephod. I am going to make a contract with you.

I will do miracles, such as have never been done before anywhere in all the earth, and all the people of Israel shall see the power of the LORD. The terrible power I will display through you. Your part of the agreement is to obey all of my commandments. You are the firstborn so whatever openeth the womb among the children of Israel, both man and beast is mine.

To you and your seed forever this is your inheritance, Levi.

To Judah, I give the things of the earth, you are king of the earth, I set the kingdom beneath the priesthood, so you must not exalt yourself against thee priesthood, which is Levi your brother.

I have sent the angel of the presence to you Judah, your eagle shall fly in gladness. To the house of Judah, joy, gladness and cheerful feasts therefore love truth and peace.

By Levi and Judah shall I the LORD of the world, show myself to every race of men that it might be fulfilled which was spoken of the LORD by the prophet saying out of Egypt have I called my sons. And I have given power unto my two witnesses, and they shall prophesy a thousand, two hundred and threescore days clothed in sackcloth. These are the two olive trees, and the two candle-sticks standing before the God of the earth.

Levi, Judah I have called you because my people is foolish, they have not known me, they are sottish children and they have none understanding, they are wise to do evil but to do good they have no knowledge.

PLANE FLEW

Levi and Judah was at an airport, waiting to board an aeroplane, the airport was filled with people going and coming, and a lot of shops.

Judah was walking around when he fell into a trance and saw a store called THE KING OF THE BIRD'S, filled with a lot of products and people, there was a picture of a yellow eagle on the door, but for some reason that picture stayed on Judah's mind.

Levi went into the lift, he was told not to go there but he wanted to see for himself, what the inside of a lift looks like. As he went in, the door of the lift shut and the whole place went dark, Judah stayed outside but could hear Levi calling out for him.

Judah, Judah called Levi.

What's up?

Get me out of here said Levi. The whole place was dark and Levi needed the lift door open, and with a touch onto the lift button the door opened.

Looking from the window of the airport, Levi and Judah could see the aeroplane they were about to board.

It was a big plane, the colour of the plane was green and a white line going down the middle, and then Judah look up at the tail of the plane and saw the same picture of the yellow eagle.

The aeroplane was on the run way about to taxi off, but Levi looked down and had a thought that the aeroplane will not make it when trying to take off.

So Levi said to his brother let us call upon the name of Nun and they both touched their foreheads together and called upon the name of Nun, all of a sudden the aeroplane cleared and took off without any problems and they got to their destination, because it was an eagle plane it soared above the rest.

GOLDEN CALF

It was a ring given to Levi and Judah by a member of their family, it was said to them, that it was a ring to protect them, a ring for power and all they had to do was to recite an incantation everyday onto this ring.

Levi and Judah were young when these ring was given to them, they did not understand what these ring was about, gold with a picture of a bull on it.

As time went, the spirit of Nun came to Levi, explaining to him the purpose of this ring. It was a ring fashioned with a graving tool made into a molten calf, and was said these be thy gods O Israel, which brought thee up out of the land of Egypt.

And the Egyptian rose up early and offered burnt offerings and brought peace offerings and the people sat down to eat and to drink and rose up to play.

And the voice of Nun came to Levi, and said destroy this out of you and Judah's life because it is a stumbing block upon your life.

Thou shalt make thee no molten gods and worship

no other god for the LORD, whose name is Jealous is a jealous GOD.

While these rings were in their possession, things were happening to Levi and Judah that they could not understand, they would plan one thing that is of God but end up doing something that is not of God, one problem after the other, but as Levi and Judah cast the rings into the sea, they looked up into the clouds and saw a reminder which said I have not forgotten you, the covenant I made between me and the earth. The covenant of the rainbow. And it shall come to pass when the bow is in the cloud, the waters shall no more become a flood to destroy all flesh.

CHILDREN OF ABEL

Playing in the park alone, when Judah was approached by two spirits, one was the angel of GOD which showed himself at the beginning and the other was the spirit of the devil, which was the dark shadow at the door.

The spirit of GOD said to Judah, whose side are you on and Judah replied, I am on the side of the children of Abel, the child of GOD and the spirit of GOD looked at the other spirit and said, you see he said he is on the side of the children of Abel.

This spirits were on a chariot and they moved on and Judah picked up a stick and was waving it and said. I am on the side of the children of Abel, the child of GOD, the child of GOD.

HANDS IN HEAVEN

It was a busy market day, the whole place was filled with people, at the centre of the square, spiritual leaders all came to show that their gods would send rain from above. You see the whole country was without rain for a long time and all the leaders placed, their mats down and some were facing a certain direction to pray, for hours they all prayed but no rain. In the mist of all these was a young boy called Judah who looked at them all, he pick up his mat and placed it down and on his right and left, people all came with their mats also and placed it down to pray.

As everyone started to pray, Judah just looked up to heaven and started to dance and sing, praise and worship songs to the most HIGH GOD.

The more Judah danced and sang the more people looked at him, some saying, and he calls this prayer. Look at this boy, what is he doing but Judah just carried on singing and dancing, all the spiritual leaders stopped and started to laugh.

God had not aloud it to rain in this land because

everyone in that land were doing his or her own business and no one was tilling the ground of the Lord.

The clouds started to move in a way that no one had ever seen before all eyes were on Judah.

Dancing and singing Judah looked up and saw a little clear drop of water coming down from the clouds he put his arms out and a drop landed onto his open palm. No one saw that drop of water except Judah, because he knew that the God he serve is a God who has ears to hear, eyes to see and mouth to speak.

Judah danced and sang the more and than the heavens opened up and gave up what it has been holding, water came down and the people all around looked at this young boy in amazement, childrens started to run around playing with the rain, but Judah just carried on, he looked into the clouds and could see hands coming out of the clouds, as he touched the hands, Judah heard, **"This Are The Hands Of My Angels".**

Everyone soaked in water, looking at Judah and someone held his right hand while his left hand was touching the clouds. As he looked, he saw that it was Nun, who said,"Fear thou not for I am with thee, be not dismayed for I am thy God: I will strengthen thee, yea I will help thee, yea I will uphold thee with the right hand of my righteousness. Behold all they that were incensed against thee shall be ashamed and confounded, they shall be as nothing and they that strive with thee shall perish.

Thou shalt seek them, and shalt not find them, even them that contended with thee, they that war against thee shall be as nothing, and as a thing of nought. For I the LORD thy GOD will hold thy right hand, saying unto thee, fear not, I will help thee, and Nun held the hand of one person that was praying facing a certain direction and people who believed were able to touch the hands in heaven.

THREE O'CLOCK

Seven sister's road going towards Finsbury Park, with every step he took Judah would just spring up, he would go over people's head.

He was very happy and everyone was looking at him, as he was doing flips in the air he got to a very high pole and went to the top and slided down.

As he started going back home still in the air, he saw a girl pointing to a guy in a security uniform. The guy was running towards Judah and when he got to him, he said to Judah come down, and Judah replied why?

It's three o'clock said the guy in the security uniform.

Judah looked at his watch and it was five past three in the morning. So what if it is three o'clock, is it against the law to be out at this time?

The voice of Nun said to Judah that three o'clock is the time for the devil and all his host to do the evil they have planned but because you are enjoying yourself in prayer and are free, they can not work.

Your prayer's is going above the heads of people who

don't pray to the most HIGH GOD that is why they are bound, but for you, your prayer's has reached the top of the pole which is to God himself, so pray without ceasing.

You and Levi, both carry a light in your hands, and the evil one and his host wants that light. A lot of my son's and daughter's also carries this light but some knows who they are and some don't. Because of this, the evil one and his host would do anything to get that light, like feed you demoniac food, try to take your peace, bring a woman or a man who is beautiful to your eyes but their heart is poison so watch and pray that you do not fall into temptation said Nun.

Levi, Judah, the evil one and his host, sleep not except they have done mischief and their sleep is taken away unless they cause some to fall for they eat the bread of wickedness, and drink the wine of violence.

WITH A BRANCH

Knock, knock, Levi and Judah knocked on the front door but no one opened, they tried their key's again but the door was chained with the security chain at the back.

It was unusual, this door is not meant to be chained, know one is meant to be inside this house, but someone is. They look at each other and wonder how they would get inside this house.

Judah put his right arm through the letter box, he touched the chain and tried to unhook it but his arm was not long enough, so he took his arm out. Let us break this door down they said, but they knew that they would have to fix it back again and that was not on the list of jobs, Levi and Judah had to do today.

Speaking to Nun in the spirit Levi asked how to open the door, he walked along the pavement thinking and came back to Judah with a piece of string in his hand, as they were talking, the spirit of Nun said to Levi, look at that branch on the floor, pick it up, tie the string around the branch and use it to unhook the chain and the door opened.

Levi walked into the house, and went straight upstairs, but Judah took the ground floor looking inside the living room and then the kitchen, he heard Levi calling out for him.

As Judah got upstairs, two guys were in the room trying to hide, and all over the room they had planned to raise their idol the god of the trees, but their business was destroyed because of Nun.

As Levi and Judah were destroying their plans, Levi commanded the two guys also to destroy their idol and one of the guy opened the window and jumped from the second floor onto the ground and ran away while Judah held the other guy. After their god was taken out of the house the other guy begged to be set free and as he too saw an open back door he fled.

The god of the trees is all about money and greed, which destroys the life of people all around them. With the same thing that they were going to use to make money was the same thing the God of Levi and Judah used to get into the house.

MONEY

When money is involve you will see the heart of a man, he will tell his staff to tell you, come back tomorrow or call before you come and collect what is yours.

His boss has gone to pray to his god and after, he is going on a long journey but if you have the GOD of Adam, he will tell you to wait, see and in no time, the boss will be back to his business.

To the people of this world, where your money is, that is where your heart will be, but to the sons and daughters of Adam, money is just paper and metal, so your heart is with GOD.

BEGGAR

Walking down the street, he saw a man begging for money, as Judah walked towards him, he saw a female friend that he knew also, she was walking towards him and the beggar.

Three of them all met at the same point, Judah said hello to his friend and carried on walking because she was talking to the beggar, but as Judah passed both of them he looked towards the floor and saw some coins, one fifty pence and one ten pence.

He pick it up, went back to the beggar and gave it to him and said God love you. Judah put his arm around the beggar and they both walked towards the side of a street in-between two shops away from the public. The beggar looked at Judah and shook his head and with one side of his mouth he raised his top lip and said yea right.

Judah was not afraid, he repeated it again, God love you, a guy like me said the beggar, with all that I have done in my life.

With the soothing of his voice yes, yes, yes a guy like you, said Judah, only you and God knows what you have done, only a sick man needs a physician, only a sinner needs to repent.

With the authority in his voice Judah said to the beggar, look at my eyes when I am talking to you and stop looking all over the place, what you are looking for is not there.

Eyes to eyes the beggar eyes lit up as if he had seen a ghost or a prophet.

Between the eyes of Judah and the eyes of the beggar a flash of light, head went back, mouth opened the beggar was dazed.

God love you and wants you to go and tell the people what he has done for you, still in shock the beggar replied yes and Judah turned with his arm still on his shoulder.

A woman who was at the side of the road said to Judah, can you come to my house some time next week and heal my daughter.

As Judah and the beggar walked away, his female friend said to him, I see you differently, from before because of what you have just done and Judah shook his head with a smile, to say, you believe because you see.

As Levi and Judah were in their store, they noticed a man dressed in sackcloth walking pass, it became an everyday thing, so they decided to stop him, and offer him food, some clothes but he declined it and walked off. One thing about this guy was that with all that he might have been going through in his life and how he looked, he had peace in his eyes that passeth all understanding and they saw him no more, only in Levi's dreams once in awhile.

Do not despise a man because of what he looks like, because some of you have attended to angels.

MAN AT THE GATE

Now Levi and Judah were just about to drive out of the temple, after the hour of prayer, when they were stopped by a man standing at the gate.

Is it well they asked him and he replied, home, I would like to go.

I am waiting to see if someone could give me a lift home.

Where is home Levi asked?

Just a way yonder he replied.

As the man got into the car, Judah moved to the back seat and the man sat on the passenger side and introduced himself as Omar.

I am Levi and this is my younger brother Judah, and as the conversation carried on between Omar and Levi, Judah was just listen-in. Omar said that he was married and when his wife noticed that his sickness could be seen by all, she walked out of his life.

After droping Omar home, Levi and Judah was on their way home when they remembered that, Omar sat with the pastor and the men of status in the temple. But as weeks went by they noticed that a man who sat and was in the mist of the men of status was now sitting at the back with the common men because of his sickness.

The men of status who use to say hello to Omar, now just walk pass him, like he was not there.

Sitting at the back in the temple, Levi and Judah walked towards Omar and sat next to him, while in the temple everyone else was greeting the pastor, catching up on the weekly talk, and even making business deals, but away from the eyes of people, Levi and Judah asked Omar, would he mind if they prayed for him?.

All three joined hands and a short prayer was made to the most HIGH GOD.

Another day at the temple, when the pastor came onto the altar to preach and said, we have a bunch of Somalia's, who came into this church and held everyone to ransom. We do not like prayer contractor's in this place, who uses this temple as a platform for themselves and do not give this house or the men of status any recognition.

While in the temple Levi and Judah, saw Omar walking around, his sickness was no more. They thanks THE GOD of Abraham, Isaac, Jacob, Levi and Judah for his healing.

Judah was walking when he met Omar, who said to him that he would like to see both Levi and Judah together, so that he could give them something. When Judah saw Levi and told him what Omar had said, Levi said to Judah, do not take anything from him because silver and gold we gave not to him. What God gave him was what he needed, which was healing.

And the words of Nun which said, what so ever you do in word or deed, do all in the name of the Lord Jesus, giving thanks to God and the father by him.

BRETHREN

And when their brethren saw that the love of Nun was upon Levi and Judah, they hated them the more.

Let us sell them to Pharaoh as slaves and see what would become of their dreams, their business and their lives.

Levi and Judah was sold to Pharaoh, who was using the grace upon their lives to run his business.

Pharaoh flaunted expensive cars, women, talked about houses and business he has bought, tried to entice Levi and Judah towards him and his host, they even placed their charm in Levi and Judah's business so that they can reduces their income to less than a few pence a day, but all that did not impress Levi or Judah. The dream that Nun placed on them was more important than the enjoyment of the flesh.

I have moved you away from them, for a reason, they would come back to you but you must not go back to them said Nun.

BUSINESS

Stare up into the skies, Judah put out his right arm and a bird, strong and large, this bird was beautiful, it is black and white with a grey, brown head. Black colour around it's neck and yellow from it's chest down to his belly, this bird looked like a king, it even had it's own crown.

You see, you don't choose this bird but he chose Judah. It came to Judah like a song in his dream.

Bow down
Bow down
Bow down
Bow down to you LORD
I just want to bow down
Bow down to you LORD.

He bowed his head down showing Judah his crown in honour this Eagle bird landed onto his arm, he moved his arm close to his chest and the bird laid his head upon it and Judah said the Eagle is in my heart.

Tuck away in the back street of London road, flown

in by the king of the birds an Eagle was placed on the high street.

It was the eve of the opening of their store and they called their family members to come and give thanks to God for this blessing.

As the business door opened family members brought, friends and members of a church to the opening but on known to Levi and Judah not all were pleased with them.

A so called deacon came towards Levi and Judah, asking if they have told the pastor of the church about this business?

But they replied, no why should we, the pastor job is to preach not to do business said Levi. The pastor would hear about this the deacon said, and they prayed upon the business.

Time went by, Levi and Judah just carried on with their business until one day when they came in to find an ocean on the shop floor, looking for a broken pipe to see if there was a leak but none. They cleaned it up and it was business as usual.

Levi was at the store one day when a member of the family came to the store, she walked around looking at the products on the shelves and as she walked around dust from her hands was scattered onto the floor, Levi saw but he kept quiet and told Judah when he came.

Nun drew us out of many waters, he delivered us from the strong enemy and from them which hated us.

A man came into the store and asked for a can of air freshen, Levi and Judah were behind the counter, then the customer said to Levi, is this your son, referring to

Judah, and Levi said no he is my brother, same mother and father.

I can now see it by your eyes said the customer, it's amazing to see brothers together even in business, because the young ones of today don't want to do it. Keep it up he said and he looked towards Levi, it is because of you.

People or brothers do not work together because they do not trust themselves, they don't know why God put them together.

Even though it was summer outside, the store was cold, it felt like you were in a freezer, because of what the evil ones did, people would walk pass the store, as if it did not exist. People who some time walked pass on a daily bases would come in and say, how long has this store been here, we notice the stores next door but we did not know that this store was here, but Levi and Judah just carried on communicating with Nun, than one day when a customer came in and said, your store is so peaceful, I see Angels on the ceiling.

With all the conspiracy again Levi and Judah the presents of Nun was with them.

WATER

And the evil ones took things like, business leaflets, products from the business, names, anything that could represent Levi, Judah and their business in the spiritual realm and they poured water from their vial onto these materials of Levi and Judah burying it under the sea and it became as the blood of a dead man, but that blood cryest from the bottomless pit, onto Nun, telling him what the evil ones were up too. The eyes of Nun are in every place, beholding the evil and the good.

Many men had died from this type of water because it was bitter water.

The evil ones tried to use water to destroy Levi and Judah, but just like Noah, they were in their own ark for eight years and stayed in until Nun said, there is land. Because of the peace that passeth all understanding above Levi, Judah and all that they own, they were covered with the blood of the Lamb.

RICH MAN

The ground of a certain rich man brought forth plentifully, and he thought within himself, saying, what shall I do because I have no room where to bestow my fruits?

And he said, this will I do, I will pull down my barns, and build greater and there will I bestow all my fruits and my goods. And I will say to my soul, Soul, thou hast much goods laid up for many years, take thine ease, eat, drink and be merry.

But God said unto him. Thou fool, this night thy soul shall be required of thee, then whose shall those things be which thou hast provided?

So is he that layeth up treasure for himself, and is not rich toward God.

For years Levi went to pick up stock from a wholesaler, he asked about stock which the wholesaler could not sell, to sell it to him at a reduce price, come back next week the rich man said and I will give you a list of all the stock I can't sell at a reduce price.

Weeks, month and years went by but the rich man

just carried on moving the days, putting up his prices when he saw Levi, and telling his brothers to set up shop close to Levi and Judah. As Levi parked around the back of the rich man barn, he saw him and his staff placing all the stock which they could not sell into a skip and binned.

The rich man then said to Levi, as from next week do not come to this small barn, I have built a bigger one with more stock.

As Levi went to buy stock one day, he drove towards the big barn and saw smoke rising up to heaven, it was even broadcast on the news, the rich man big barn was no more.

Even the little, that Levi and Judah has, the rich man covetousness, brought him back to his beginning.

MY PEOPLE

My people think they are doing us evil by not coming to buy from our business, they are only putting their sons and daughters into salvery for another one to forty years.

EGYPTIAN

O you Egytian, how long are your eyes going to be shut, don't you know I have opened your eyes long ago.

I sent my prophets to you but you preferred, men with sweet words, rabbis who receive praise in the market place, with fine attire.

You, know that I sent my prophets to speak my words to you but you choose to shut your eyes and ears to my words, O you Egyptian.

SABBATH DAY

Sunday Eight Forty in the morning, Levi was driving and Judah was sitting at the passenger side of the car, it was a beautiful day for driving. As they were on their way to church, they came towards a traffic light, the light turned red and Levi pressed the breaks, all of a sudden the car swerve but GOD helped Levi to bring it under control.

This was a battle that Levi and Judah were going through, not a battle of the flesh but of the spirit, their warfare are not carnal, but mighty through God to the pulling down of strong holds. On their way Levi and Judah started blowing the trumpet of war and as they got inside the church the intruder alarm was set off, the place was filled with a lot of people.

You see a church is a place for people to get spiritual answers to the probelms they are facing in life, but in this church the so called man of god was not giving spiritual answers to people but talked more about himself, his family, and more about money.

This pastor loved to show what he is about, one day

he brought a car, the top of the range car into the church for all to see, and buy.

Levi and Judah looked at each other and said what is this pastor doing. At that moment the voice of Nun said. My house is a house of prayer's but you have made it a den of thives.

Hearken not unto the words of the prophets that prophesy unto you, they make you vain, they speak a vision of their own heart and not out of the mouth of the Lord.

They say still unto them that despise me, the Lord hath said. Ye shall have peace and they say unto every one that walketh after the imagination of his own heart, no evil shall come upon you.

I have not sent these prophets, yet they ran, I have not spoken to them, yet they prophesied. They want my people to forget my name by their dreams but if they had stood in my counsel and had caused my people to hear my words, then they should have turned them from their evil ways and from the evil of their doings.

As time went by Levi said to Judah, we need to call upon the name of Nun in this place, so they started calling upon the name of Nun and some of the people there fall asleep, some coughed, some sneezed, even babies started crying. The calling of the name of Nun was releasing them from their burdens, and also binding some to sleep, the demon in them were leaving. As Levi and Judah called on the name of Nun, cold air went past them.

When Levi and Judah drew near and was in the mist of their enemies, they kept by themselves, and While they called on the name of Nun they seat down, with their hands over their faces, their mouths moving but people around could not hear a sound.

Around Levi and Judah was a spiritual smoke when they prayed, this smoke had the power to bind any demon or his human host.

That is why all the demonic spirit in that place strived to escape from the smoke. As a believer you will get spiritual attack if you call upon the name of Jesus Christ but do not give up because you will overcome.

While they prayed an order by the demon head of that place was sent out to follow Levi and Judah and a hit was upon their life but because they called and prayed in the name and the blood of Jesus Christ all the attacks came to nothing, for who so ever will save his life shall lose it and who so ever will lose his life for my sake shall find it.

If you are in a church or somewhere and you just start getting an headache, it is possible that someone is trying to take the anointing that is on your head. some time those headaches are arrows of stones that has been shot at you. To put sickness on you, for example cancer which is a malignant growth, any evil that gradually destroys.

Once sickness has been put on someone and if you stop praying for thirty days or more, the evil one can overpower you as a believer, because he wants to weaken you in the flesh and also in the spirit, that is why they tried to stop Daniel, Shadrach, Meshach and Abed-nego from praying and serve the gods of that land, but because they refused, they were cast into the lions den and also put into the fire.

Then the presidents and princes sought to find occasion against Daniel concerning the kingdom, but they could find none occasion nor fault, for as much as he was faithful, neither was there any error or fault found in him.

Then said these men, we shall not find any occasion against this Daniel, except we find it against him concerning the law of his God.

Then these presidents and princes assembled together to the king, and said thus unto him, king Darius, live for ever.

All the presidents of the kingdom, the governors, and the princes, the counsellers, and the captains, have consulted together to establish a royal statute, and to make a firm decree, that who so ever shall ask a petition of any God or man for thirty days, save of thee, o king, he shall be cast into the den of lions.

Now when Daniel knew that the decree as gone out, he went into his house, kneeled upon his knees, three times a day and prayed, and gave thanks before his God, as he did aforetime.

This men now told the king, who because of the law of the land and the decree cast Daniel into the den of lions, and the lions did not even touched Daniel, because he still prayed even in the den.

Also Shadrach, Meshach and Abed-nego, these men o king have not regarded thee, they serve not thy gods, nor worship the golden image which thou hast set up.

Then the king, Nebuchadnezzar commanded to bring these men and he asked, do not ye serve my gods, nor worship the golden image which I have set up?

Shadrach, Meshach and Abed-nego, answered the king, we are not careful to answer thee in this matter.

If it be so, our God whom we serve is able to deliver

us from the burning fiery furnace, and he will deliver us out of thine hand, o king.

But if not, be it known unto thee, o king, that we will not serve thy gods, nor worship the golden image which thou hast set up.

And the king commanded, his most mighty men that were in his army to bind Shadrach, Meshach and Abed-nego, and to cast them into the burning fiery furnace. But when they were cast into the midst of the burning fiery furnace, God came and loose them and the fire did not hurt them.

And the king's said. Blessed be the God of Daniel, Shadrach, Meshach, and Abed-nego, who hath sent his Angel, and delivered his servants that trusted in him, and have changed the king's word, and yielded their bodies, that they might not serve nor worship any gods, except their own GOD.

O MAN OF GOD

O man of GOD, why have you gone so low, to let a mule into my house, sit, park and give off his gas, don't you know this is my temple.

How would you like it, if I put that mule in your house, you preach about taking my people out of poverty but you are putting them into it the more.

Buy now, pay later or monthly, O man of God, why are you letting money change hands in my house, as I said my house is a house of prayers.

STOREHOUSE

Listen to this saying Levi and Judah, will a man rob God? Yet ye have robbed me. But ye say, wherein have we robbed thee? In tithes and offerings.

Ye are cursed with a curse, for ye have robbed me, even this whole nation. Bring ye all the tithes into the storehouse, that there may be meat in mine house, and prove me now herewith, saith the LORD of hosts, if I will not open you the windows of heaven, and pour you out a blessing, that there shall not be room enough to receive it.

And I will rebuke the devourer for your sakes, and he shall not destroy the fruits of your ground, neither shall your vine cast her fruit before the time in the field, saith the LORD of hosts.

The so called men of God of your generation has turned this saying around, to fill their own pockets, they use it because they know, that tithing is a commandment I gave to Israel and that ten percent of your first fruits belongs to me your GOD.

But Nun we have bought your tithes willingly from

our heart into your storehouse, so why has the devourer come against our ground.

Yes, you gave your tithes willingly from your heart, but the ground that you placed it on was not a fruitful field, it is filled with sorcerers, adulterers, swearers, those that oppress the hireling in his wages and that turn aside the stranger from his right.

Every time the tithes and offerings bucket comes around, and you or anybody in that place, put his or her tithes and offerings into it or take his or her tithes and offerings and placed it on **that** altar which I have not ordain, you or them, have just made a covenant with the gods of **that** place. The so called men of God of that place, don't fear me. The LORD of hosts, I have not ordain that field so you or anybody in that place cannot grow. The only people, who will grow are the so called men of God and their host, but their prosperity will only last for a short time.

Levi, Judah that tithes and offering which was given on that altar, which I did not ordain, should have been given to the widows, the fatherless, the poor as alms. I don't need money, what I need from people is obedience and not sacrifice.

Make sure you give your tithes and offering in a church ordain by God and not by man, because that is the only way your seed will grow.

ARE YOU A CHRISTIAN

Levi and Judah has been calling upon the name of Nun for over fifteen months in the church and at the end of the service, they were approached by two ladies.

One went to Levi and asked how can you hear what the pastor is saying when you are always praying and Levi said to her, your ears are for hearing and she asked, are you and your brother christians, yes replied Levi. But you don't act like all the other christians in this church, she said. Not everyone in church are christians replied Levi.

She than said thank you for your prayers and walked off.

It was another day at the church when Levi and Judah was just about to leave. When they were stopped by two men who said, that they wanted to talk to them, so Levi and Judah went outside.

The men introduced themselves as ministers of the church and said that they have noticed that Levi, or Judah don't take part in what is going on in the church, that they come, sit down and start praying until the end of the services and then leave. That the prayers of Levi and

Judah is disturbing the other people and that they needed to take part in what the church is doing. For example, if they are singing in church, Levi and Judah should sing also, if they are praying, Levi and Judah should also pray and so on.

We have people praying in a different room while the service is taking place said one of the minister, and why are you praying.

Levi looked at him and said you are a minister of God, go to God and ask why this guys are praying, maybe God would tell you.

What would you like us to do now asked Judah, stop praying they said.

We cannot stop praying replied Levi and Judah, you cannot stop the Holy Spirit from manifesting and the two ministers walked off.

They shall put you out of the synagogues, yea the time cometh that who so ever killeth you will think that he doeth God service.

Keep thy foot when thou goest to the house of God, and be more ready to hear than to give the sacrifice of fools, for they consider not that they do evil.

Just has they got home, Judah was cleaning his fish tank when the words of Nun came to him. They are not your brothers or sisters, what do you mean Nun, Judah said.

Look at one of my book Matthew 12:46-50, I said who are my brothers? Then I pointed to my disciples and said look! here are my mother and my brothers?

Whoever does what my father in heaven wants him to do is my brother, my sister and my mother.

O MIGHTY MAN

O why broader yourself in mischief, O mighty man, the glory of the Lord was upon thou but you abused it. You tried the fatherless, the widows with the back of your hands. They needed food, you gave them stone, they needed a touch of care, you gave them a whipping, they knocked at your door daily for help but you kept it locked.

You forgot that there is one greater than you who has no respecter of persons, you forgot that you too have to knock on a door greater than yourself and all what you have is all vanity.

There would be a time when your prosperity can not save you. So who would you turn to, the work of your own hands. You forgot your life is but one breath. Open your eyes, heart and see what the Lord wants you to do and store up treasure in heaven not on earth, O mighty man.

MONITOR

Judah there is a painting on your wall that you need to take down, said Nun because that is how they are monitoring you and Levi.

As they went up the stairs and got onto the landing to the rooms, there was a big painting on the wall and as Levi walked pass, Judah looked at the painting and the eyes in the painting moved.

He called Levi and said look at this and he moved the painting along the wall and saw a camera, as he was about to take it down, then Precious came onto the landing and said, we should not take down the painting, an argument broke out between Judah and their family member, so Judah walked away but she did not want to stop arguing, so Levi pick her up and shut her in a room.

Let me out she shouted, let me out.

After a few minutes Judah came back and said to Precious, so you have been monitoring Levi and I all this time and all for what said Judah, Is it all for money and she replied yes.

As Judah walked away he fell into a trance, he saw his

nephew and embraced him, but his nephew said, uncle. Mum and Dad has told him, his brother and their sister not to talk to you or uncle Levi, but just has he finished talking his Dad came to Judah and said, I have told you not to talk to my children and when you see them just walk on bye and Judah replied, do you think you and I are made from the same piece of cloth and he said what do you mean.

Your god says to you, when you see your brother or sister, walk pass them like you don't know them. But my God says when you see your brother or sister, kiss, embrace, show love to him or her and then go your way. Judah came back to his sense and the words of Nun which saids.

He that saith he is in the light, and hateth his brother, is in darkness even until now. He that loveth his brother abideth in the light and there is none occasion of stumbling in him.

But he that hateth his brother is in darkness, and walketh in darkness, and knoweth not whither he goeth, because that darkness hath blinded his eyes.

One day when Levi and Judah were driving, they saw their nephew at a bus stop, so they picked him up and took him to the library were he was going, they gave him a bag which had, two t-shirts and a hat. The t-shirts were for him, his younger brother and the hat was for their sister.

The next day it was Judah's birthday, Levi and him were at Judah house having a barbecue allowing the smoke to reach up to heaven for a thanksgiving offering. The smell of barbecue chicken even got the neighbours dogs barking, when the door bell went. Judah opened the garden door and saw Precious, her husband and their daughter.

After awhile Precious and her family left, that night Levi and Judah both had a spiritual attack, Levi had pains on one side of his body. Levi and Judah both had headaches, pain around their chest.

Two weeks later, Judah was driving when he saw his youngest nephew walking, as he pulled over and asked him were he was going, he replied home. Come I will give you a lift said Judah, his nephew look at him and said no and shook his head. Judah asked why, which he replied, his mum told his brother off for getting into the car and she has told all of her children not to get into your cars.

That night a message was left on Judah's phone by their father which said, Hello Judah, how are things, Levi how is he, I phoned to say that please don't stay at the bus stop to pick my children in god's name and tell Levi also, let no one pick them up, don't say hello to them, please don't wait for them and if you see them don't say hello to them, please in god's name thanks.

FLY ON THE WALL

It was not the time of year, that flies should be around, but for some reason, Levi and Judah would notice them around. Time went by when Levi and Judah, would notice flies on the wall, sometimes in the middle of the night, sometimes they would hear the noise but could not see the fly.

When they prayed the flies would disappear, and sometimes would come back after they prayed. What can it be they wonder.

The evil ones can use dogs, cats, spiders, flies to carry witchcrafts messages, the king of Babylon stood at the parting of the way, to use divination he made his arrows bright, he consulted with images, he looked in the liver but it shall be a false divination in their sight to them that have sworn oaths. I will call to remembrance their iniquity said NUN.

WHILE MEN SLEPT

Levi and Judah were walking through a street, when they saw a little girl playing with paint outside of her house, she had paint on her legs and was just about to put her hands into the paint container, when Levi and Judah stopped her, this little girl was about the age of two years old.

Levi and Judah knocked on the door of the little girl house to see if someone was in, but the door just pushed open and they heard people talking. It sounds like praying said Levi, so the little girl took Levi and Judah hands and led them into the house.

In the house was the girl parents and a few other people all praying, so Levi and Judah said Amen at the end of the prayer not knowing what the prayer was about.

The little girl's mum, came towards Levi and Judah and said to them, when are you going to come and work for us, give up your jobs and come.

They looked at the mum of the little girl and said to her, you are a very wicked and evil person, how can we leave the job, GOD as placed on us, to work for you, she looked at them in amazement and her countenance changed, she and the other people carried on praying, trying to change their minds because Levi and Judah was not there in the flesh but in the spirit. While men slept, his enemy came and sowed tares among the wheat and went his way.

With the power of Nun in them, Levi and Judah opened their mouths and at first, words could not come out, because it felt like someone or something held their tongues and a heaviness of weight was on their heads, they struggled to set their heads free. But by calling upon the name of Nun from within, they were free. As they started to send fire and brimstone upon that gathering everyone fled.

This was not the first time that Levi or Judah, has been called in the spirit, and if a king, called Saul could seek a woman that hath a familar spirit so that he could inquire of her to call up the spirit of Samuel the prophet who was asleep (DEAD) in those time, what is stopping people of this generation.

And when Saul inquired of the LORD, the Lord answered him not, neither by dreams, nor by U-rim, nor by prophets. When people do things like that it is because God has left them.

JEZEBAL

Not with standing, I have a few things against the churches of today said Nun, because thou sufferest that woman Jezebal, which calleth herself a prophetess to teach and to seduce my servants to commit fornication and to eat things sacrificed unto idols, you let her come unto the pulpit dressed in purple and beautiful colours, she is decked in gold and precious stones and pearls.

As Judah walked into the hall, someone tapped him on his shoulder, he was just about to turn around when a guy came and pushed him and said, carry on walking, I will tell you when you get outside.

That person who tapped your shoulder was Jezebal, the woman Nun has told you and Levi about and all she has to do is take someone's hair or belongings and can seduce that person.

Just about to go inside the church, when Judah looked at a side door, where he saw a staircase going up and a lot of women dancing, they were lining up to go up the stair.

Judah looked to his right but the guy had disappear

and he heard the voice of Nun which said, all this women are just about to be like Jezebal, I have given her time but she repented not, she has allowed my daughter's to come into my temple dress like whores, showing flesh they do not honour their head.

She sitteth upon many waters, and some people see her as a beautiful temple in the middle of the ocean, kings of the earth have committed fornication and the inhabitants of the earth have been made drunk with the wine of her fornication.

She is beautiful to look upon but inside of her are dead men bones.

PHARAOH

Levi told Judah that he saw the devil and on the devil's chest he had a crown. As Levi and Judah were talking a big fat guy started talking to Levi and they started to argue.

Judah, just give me a few minutes said Levi, I just want to talk to this guy and they moved away from Judah.

As they were arguing, they started moving further away from Judah and then another guy, who was much older than the first came into the conversation which Levi and the fat guy were having. All three carried on the argument, moving further away from Judah.

The two guys were leading Levi somewhere, first through a field. Has Judah saw this, he ran after them and the big guy tried to stop him, so they started to fight, people were gathering around them and some were following Levi and the older guy, but Judah kept one eye on the older guy and Levi, he saw that they went behind a building, so he quickly knocked the big guy out and ran around the building where he saw Levi and the other guy.

The old guy wanted to fight Levi but Levi did not want too, so when Judah came over, the older guy started running away, and Judah now said to Levi, did you not see what just happened, you were telling me about the devil, who had a crown and the next thing two guys wanted to fight you.

The devil was trying to take your crown which Nun has placed upon you, just like the two angels in dark garment at the beginning, who wanted us to open the door for them, so that they could come in.

POLICE MEN

As they were in a store doing some shopping, Levi and Judah noticed that four police men were in the store talking between themselves.

The police men took the store manager outside and said something to him and when the store manager came back into the store, he started looking at Levi and Judah, but they just carried on shopping.

The store manager quickly went to the back of the store and after a few minutes came back onto the shopfloor and was watching everywhere they went.

Judah said to Levi, you know that the police are watching us and they are waiting outside to jump on us, how are we going to get out of this store, what have we done?

Levi now said, the enemy has set a trap and he wants us to take the blame, we will call upon the name of Nun and he would show us a way.

And they called upon the name of Nun, destroying any arrow sent towards them and to shut the eyes of the police men when they are going out.

As Levi and Judah came out of the store, they walked towards their car when one of the police men called them, as they turned around to him, his co-worker called him and said, don't waste your time with them let them go, the guys we want are inside and they told Levi and Judah to go.

BRO, HE IS MY HERO

Judah was woken up by a noise around six thirty in the morning, it sounded like something was on top of the roof, so he got out of bed and looked outside trying to see if he could see anything but nothing. Judah now went back to bed.

A few seconds later he heard the noise again and he got up and went to the back room, where he found a bird inside the room, flying and trying to get out. I have not opened the window nor left it open said Judah to himself, so how did this bird get in here.

Judah left the room, closed the door and called Levi on the phone explaining to him what he just saw. Levi told Judah to come and pick him up which he did.

When Levi came he opened the door to the back room and saw the bird, flying, hitting the window trying to get out, then Levi and Judah went into the room and shut the door behind them.

When the bird saw that they both were in the room, it turned around and flew towards them trying to attack them, it would fly towards them with his foots or beak wide open ready to take their eyes out, but with the swiftness of Levi and Judah, they would move out of the way.

As time went on they realised that this bird did not come into this house through an open door or window, but only through the spiritual realm and not for peace but for destruction.

This bird came while man slept but forgot that when a house calls upon the name of Nun without ceasing, the blood of the Lamb is upon that house. Whatever has been sent by air, water, earth, day or night would be destroyed by fire, which it was.

Then Judah remembered a dream he had over a year ago when someone gave him a present. The present was of an animal which looks like a rat with wings, so he took it home opened the cage and the animal came out, and ran under the belfast kitchen sink.

After a period of time, Judah told Levi about the present and where the animal was, so they decided to catch it and put it back into the cage but everytime they tried to catch it, it flew away.

Judah moved to one end of the room with a shoe box in his hand and Levi was at the other end. When the animal flew towards Judah, he hit it with the cover of the shoe box and it flew towards Levi and he hit it back towards Judah.

After awhile of hitting this animal, like that, Judah opened the shoe box and caught it and then he woke up.

A friend loveth at all times and a brother is born for adversity.

WHAT I THINK OF YOU
AND YOUR GOD

Judah was alone at the store one day when a lady, their neighbour who has a store a few doors from them, came in and asked, if Judah could change some notes for her, but Judah did not have any change and said to her that he was waiting for Levi to come so that he could go to the bank.

Judah perceived that the money she brought was demoniac. The lady then said to Judah if he could help her, that she is finding it hard in her store, the rent and everything is too much and if Judah could tell her what they are doing in their store.

Judah looked at her and said, I would not know, Levi is the best person to speak too. She then started to talk to Judah about her children and the school that they are attending, but as she was speaking, she was looking into the eyes of Judah and winking. Judah tried not to look at her eyes because he perceived she was trying to bewitch him.

After a few minutes of her leaving the store, Judah started to have an headache, he thought about it for a minute or two and it came to his mind, that he was fine before this lady came in and when she left, he started to have an headache.

Judah started calling upon the name of Nun at that time every knees shall bow, things in heaven, on earth and under the earth. Every tongue shall confess that Nun is Lord, to the glory of God the father.

Judah started to vomit into the bin next to him and his head got warmer and his eyes opened and he looked at the bin and said, that is what I think of you and your god.

DELIVERANCE

Shut in two different rooms to the outside world, it was time for the deliverance of Levi and Judah.

All because they stayed in prayer to the LORD of lords, which was the master key to life for the believer.

Surely there is no enchantment against Jacob, neither is there any divination against Israel, according to this time it shall be said of Jacob and of Israel, what hath GOD wrought, it shall also be said of Levi and Judah, what hath GOD wrought because Jacob and Israel are one, also Levi and Judah are one in the blood of the Lamb.

Days went by when Levi and Judah fasted without food and water, sometimes three, four, five, six, seven or more days only to break, for a day or two and as a drop of water touched their lips, life came back to their bodies, for months they fasted and went to work, only because Nun gave them the strength to accomplish it.

They started to vomit not what they had just eaten, but a bitter lime water to the taste, with something inside, which looks like blood sometimes and little white crystals.

Their body shocked like a volt of power just went through them, their lungs was set on fire, the more water they drank and took a deep breath, the more the blood bitter lime water and little white crystals came out.

The more they sang and worship, commanding every demoniac deposit in them to come out in Jesus name by air or liquid through the opening in their body, the more they were been delivered.

Self deliverance is possible, you don't need to go from place to place looking for help, believe in your father which is in heaven and he would deliver you when the time is right but you have to live an Holy Life and I repeat you have to live an Holy Life.

And these signs shall follow them that believe. In my name shall they cast out devils, they shall speak with new tongues. They shall take up serpents and if they drink any deadly thing, it shall not hurt them, they shall lay hands on the sick and they shall recover.

They passed out wind from their buttock, life moved away from their legs, to stand was impossible sometimes but that was part of their deliverance.

All because of the enemy within, which was given to them as holy communion in quote. The bottom line for a bona fide believers is prayer.

MY LORD SAID OWE NO MAN NOTHING BUT LOVE

Lord your principles does work, thou knowest. You said owe no man nothing but love, this principle gives me peace of mind.

Before I knew who I am in Christ, people tried to out my life, now that I know who I am in Christ, I owe no man nothing but love.

I bought a house people dislike it, but I owe no man nothing but love. I started a business but all my business associate dislike me but I owe no man nothing but love. I went to one of the biggest supplier of stock in the country, I humbled myself to buy stock. He asked for a huge sum, first time order, I collected the sum for him, the second time I went back to pick up stock with cash he reqiured, he refused and drove me away, I owe no man nothing but love.

I was forced to find another supplier when he noticed that every week I came to buy he put up his prices, sometimes one hundred percent but I owe no man nothing but love.

The price you gave to your brothers is not the same you gave me, but I owe no man nothing but love. I know you not but you went to sorcery, you've forgotten to read your bible Numbers 23:23 there is no sorcery against Jacob, no divination against Israel, it will now be said of Jacob and of Israel, see what God has done, I owe no man nothing but love.

I know you not but you send demons to me at night to out my life, don't you read your bible no weapon formed against me will ever prosper, I owe no man nothing but love.

Am a young man running and minding my business, you dislike it but I owe no man nothing but love. I talk you dislike it, I walk you dislike it, I dance you dislike it, I know you not but I did you favours, you dislike it, I refuse to be boxed in, you dislike it, you know what my Lord said owe no man nothing but love.

PRAYER

O LORD my GOD, I thank you for the brother that you gave me, without you LORD in my life what would my life be. If only the world knew why you put different people in the same family, they would not fight against each other but for me you gave me a brother for peace, a rock, a word of wisdom when I wanted to do my own thing.

When everyone forsook me, he was still there, if only Cain knew why you gave him Abel as a brother, he would not have killed him.

I pray O LORD that you remove the spirit of Cain which is upon some of my brothers of this generation, so that they too can have the love that Levi and Judah has, the love of a brother.

I know that they have gone astray but please unblock their heart of stone, so that they can return onto you LORD.

Our father's were sent away because of their sins, but now their sons and daughters gather together from the east to the west by your word, rejoicing because we are coming home to you.

The blood of our father Abel which callest from the ground has asked for forgiveness because they know not what they are doing, the life is in the blood.

The blood that was in Abel the blood of Jesus Christ our LORD and saviour, I placed upon my brother's and sister's of this generation, the prayer of Levi and Judah has ended. AMEN.

CONCLUSION

They that trust in the Lord shall be as mount Zion, which cannot be removed, but abideth forever, for the rod of the wicked shall not rest upon the lot of the righteous, lest the righteous put forth their hands unto iniquity.

The one thing a child of GOD needs to do is to pray, how can a son talk to his father, except he communicate with him. So prayer is the only way a believer can communicate with GOD.

As you have read this book, you would have noticed that Levi and Judah communicated with their father, it is not all in talking but also in singing, dancing, in deeds, and giving in alms. Even making someone smile that could be your prayer.

The evil one meant it for evil but all things work together for the good of those who love the Lord, GOD. AMEN.